Garden City

Garbatella

THE VILLAGE IN ROME

A TRAVEL PHOTO ART BOOK

LAINE CUNNINGHAM

Garden City Garbatella

The Village in Rome

A Travel Photo Art Book

Published by Sun Dogs Creations
Changing the World One Book at a Time
Print ISBN: 9781946732989

Cover Design by Angel Leya

Copyright © 2019 Laine Cunningham

All rights reserved. No part of this book may be reproduced in any form or by any means, electronic, mechanical, digital, photocopying or recording, except for the inclusion in a review, without permission in writing from the publisher.

THE TRAVEL PHOTO ART SERIES

Bikes of Berlin
Necropolises of New Orleans I & II
Ruins of Rome I & II
Ancients of Assisi I & II
Panoramas of Portugal
Nuances of New York
Glimpses of Germany
Impressions of Italy
Altitudes of the Alps
Knights Through the Ages
Coast of California
Utopia of the Unicorn
Flourishes of France
Portraits of Paris
Tableaus of Tbilisi
Grandeur in the Republic of Georgia
Paragons of Prague
Hidden Prague
Lidice Lives
Along the Via Appia
The Pillars of the Bohemian Paradise
Terezín and Theresienstadt

BEVELED

FLOCK

LILIUM

OLD SOCIAL

PRIVATE JUNGLE

RED-EYE

SNUG

TRAIL GUIDE

TUNNEL

FOUNTAIN

HAMLET

GRAFFITI

TURRET

VAN DYKE

RADIAL

PUNK ROCK

ASYMMETRY

ALTOGETHER

RUFFLES

CIRCUS

COLUMBARY

HEADING HOME

IMPRESSIONIST

CITY VILLA

BAGUA

BELVEDERE

CORNER MADONNA

JOURNEY'S END

LANTERN

RIFT

PISA

PALLADIAN

SHAMROCK

COUNTRY MANOR

ABOUT THE AUTHOR

Laine Cunningham leads readers around the world. *The Family Made of Dust* is set in the Australian Outback, while *Reparation* is a novel of the American Great Plains. Her travel memoir *Woman Alone* appeals to fans of *Wild* and *Eat Pray Love*.

NOVELS BY
LAINE CUNNINGHAM

The Family Made of Dust

Beloved

Reparation

OTHER BOOKS BY
LAINE CUNNINGHAM

*Woman Alone: A Six-Month Journey
Through the Australian Outback*

On the Wallaby Track

Seven Sisters: Spiritual Messages from Aboriginal Australia

Writing While Female or Black or Gay

The Zen of Travel
The Zen of Gardening
Zen in the Stable
The Zen of Chocolate
The Zen of Dogs

Bikes of Berlin
Necropolises of New Orleans I & II
Ruins of Rome I & II
Ancients of Assisi I & II
Panoramas of Portugal
Nuances of New York
Glimpses of Germany
Impressions of Italy
Altitudes of the Alps
Knights Through the Ages
Coast of California
Utopia of the Unicorn
Flourishes of France
Portraits of Paris
Tableaus of Tbilisi
Grandeur in the Republic of Georgia
Paragons of Prague
Hidden Prague
Lidice Lives
Along the Via Appia
The Pillars of the Bohemian Paradise
Terezín and Theresienstadt

www.ingramcontent.com/pod-product-compliance
Lightning Source LLC
Chambersburg PA
CBHW041321110526
44591CB00021B/2859